PATIENCE

Patience

Taking Time in an
Age of Acceleration

Akiko Busch

STERLING

New York / London
www.sterlingpublishing.com

STERLING and the distinctive Sterling logo are registered
trademarks of Sterling Publishing Co., Inc.

Library of Congress Cataloging-in-Publication Data Available

10 9 8 7 6 5 4 3 2 1

Published by Sterling Publishing Co., Inc.
387 Park Avenue South, New York, NY 10016
© 2010 by Akiko Busch
Distributed in Canada by Sterling Publishing
c/o Canadian Manda Group, 165 Dufferin Street
Toronto, Ontario, Canada M6K 3H6

Sterling ISBN 978-1-4027-6647-3

For information about custom editions, special sales,
premium and corporate purchases, please contact
Sterling Special Sales Department at 800-805-5489
or specialsales@sterlingpublishing.com.

Contents

Patience—has a quiet Outer—
Patience—Look within—
Is an Insect's futile forces
Infinites—between—

'Scaping one—against the other
Fruitlesser to fling—
Patience—is the Smile's exertion
Through the quivering—

—*Emily Dickinson* (1864)

Introduction

Every family inhabits space differently. In ours, it had to do with a sense of time. And something called the time margin.

My father had a theory about this. As a young man, he had worked at *Time* magazine when it was this country's first weekly news magazine, and later he was a war correspondent for *Life* magazine. Traveling at a moment's notice, working on deadline, and filing stories promptly were all skills he had honed to a fine art. Small wonder, then, that he did his best to pass along this keen observance of how time passed to my sister and me.

And what he most emphasized was his belief in the time margin. Whenever any of us had any place to go—to school or swimming lessons when we were children, and to summer jobs, college orientation, on trains and airplanes later on—we would receive the sermon about the time margin and how one must always leave an adequate space of time before whatever event lay ahead. The rambling discourse touched upon various points, among them life's unexpected occurrences that can cause delays: possible traffic or road construction, unforeseen weather conditions, the perils of being in a rush, the need to consider others who may be counting on you.

The time margin was a matter of honor in our family. Like children often do, I found myself translating this abstract idea into a mental image, in this case the kind of margin found on a page in my loose-leaf notebook: a narrow strip of white paper with horizontal blue lines separated by a thin, vertical red line from all the words and numbers that might be scattered across the remainder of the page.

In the intervening years, the time margin and I have become intimate friends, and our relationship has evolved in subtle and complex ways. It no longer simply precedes a date, an engagement, some departure or arrival. It goes without saying that when I am driving to the train station, or to a movie or a doctor's appointment, or have a deadline—that is, when I am getting myself to some event or meeting that has a designated hour and minute—I leave *plenty of time*.

But it is with some embarrassment that I have come to admit that the time margin also attends the lesser and more random events of my life: roasting a chicken for dinner, for example, or swimming laps, or reading. Reading? Yes, even reading, I have discovered, can use a slim margin of time before it, a little sliver of quiet space before I pick up the book. And there have been times, too, when I am anticipating an important event, that I might go so far as to leave a time margin around the time margin—which is to say, leave a bit of extra time so I am sure to have the extra time I may need. At such moments, it is even possible for the time margin to become more important than the event itself, overshadowing it and superseding it in value altogether. The time margin, I have discovered, can be an event of its own. No longer simply a prelude to experience, it becomes an experience unto itself with its own value, character, atmosphere.

As peculiar as my arrangements with the time margin may be, I have noticed that many of us, as we get older, experience similar shifts, complexities, and irregularities in our relationship to time. Time itself has become more elastic. Often compressed, elsewhere it seems to stretch out indefinitely. It operates on a new spectrum. Its character has changed. It has become less predictable, less knowable. It has its own elusive cycles. We have all the time in the world for some things and none for others. My father taught me that the time margin preceded an event, but it is clear to me that it can surround an event on all sides.

While we may inhabit time differently as we get older, it is an even more pressured exercise in this age of acceleration. With our instant–messaging, microwaved meals, and drive-through pharmacies, we operate in overdrive. "Speed shrinking" describes a new form of psychotherapy in which clients can speak with psychiatrists and psychologists in three-minute bursts for spontaneous counsel that replaces the fifty-minute hour—forget the years required for traditional analysis. Einstein famously suggested that the only reason for time is so that everything doesn't happen at once. Yet the continuous flow of information into our lives, the conviction that we can perform verbal, visual, and manual tasks simultaneously, and the fact that the average computer user keeps eight windows open at a time all put this theory to test.

I read recently that the computer industry considers the three-minute boot-up time of computers a black hole; they are trying to reduce it to thirty seconds. Hewlett-Packard researchers found that when people have to wait more than a few minutes, "it seems like an eternity." It seems we are all waiting—all of us, all the time, hurriedly, anxiously, irritably, calmly, quietly, however we choose—at commuter train stations, at bus stops, in traffic, in the checkout line, at our desks, in our kitchens, sitting on the sofa fast-forwarding through the commercials. But even the word *fast-forward* has become anachronistic, a relic of the analog age.

Percolating in response to "time poverty"—surely

a phrase particular to these times—is the Slow Movement. Slow Food, a response both to the burgers and fries of fast food and to the way we have managed to hasten traditional mealtime rituals, has set out to reestablish time-honored human patterns of growing food, buying locally, and sharing meals. Slow Travel is a way to take in foreign landscapes at a gentler pace that allows the traveler to absorb unfamiliar places, cultures, and rituals in a deeper and more sustaining way than simply dashing from one must-see landmark to another. Slow Money considers new capital markets that put preservation and restoration ahead of "extraction and consumption," while Slow Gardening is a way of observing both seasonal and personal rhythms. Rather than racing to plant expansive plots as soon as spring comes, the idea is to nurture small gardens that can be easily maintained and enjoyed—a few pots of basil and rosemary in the kitchen, say, rather than fifteen heirloom tomato plants you'll never be able to keep up with in August. And, inevitably, there is the Slow Media movement that advocates getting unplugged and unwired, paring down the e-mails and text messages, curtailing the frantic pace of social networking, disconnecting digitally in an effort to reconnect with each other, with community, and with place more directly.

Arden Reed is writing a book about what he calls "Slow Art." He tells me it is, in part, about the mystery of the visible. The ability to take in what is before our very eyes, he observes, is far more interesting than the mystery of the invisible, and he speaks of the dialogue that can be established between the viewer and the painting. Asking "how do you look at Matisse if you've been raised on MTV?" Reed goes on to suggest that "Slow Art is a transaction." As an example he cites James Turrell's installation "Backside of the Moon" on the Japanese island of Naoshima. Visitors enter a darkened room on the site of a former temple, where they sit in silence. Only after five or ten minutes, when their eyes have adjusted to the absence of light, do they begin to see points of brightness, shape, and color. "Your eyes have to get used to the dark," he says. "Slow Art is a way of understanding an image as an event."

And I realize that when I was a young girl listening to my father, the time margin was a narrow strip of white alongside, say, a book report, or columns of numbers reciting the complete multiplication tables. Now, though, it more resembles some exercise in conceptual art—inches, possibly even feet and yards of blank white space surrounding a single letter or numeral.

If there is a name to that white space, it is likely to be Patience.

The word *patience* is derived from the Latin *patiens*, meaning hardy, able, tolerant, willing to endure. And, historically, the word surely implied the kind of resilience it took to withstand suffering. "Patience," a poem of unknown authorship from the Pearl Manuscript written in the fourteenth century, begins with these lines:

Patience is a virtue, though it often may displease.

When sorrowful hearts are hurt by scorn or something else,

Long suffering can assuage them and ease the pain,

For she kills everything bad and extinguishes malice.

For if anyone could endure sorrow, happiness would follow.

"Why don't people name their children Patience anymore?" a friend of mine asks. I would guess it is because the word's traditional association with dire adversity has little appeal.

But if patience still connotes a kind of endurance, it may be less a matter of privation and hardship today and more a matter of how we inhabit time, both as that deeper kind of waiting we all engage in—waiting to say the right thing at the right moment, waiting for a child to grow, waiting for clarity about something you are unsure of—and as a day-to-day endeavor: catching trains, returning phone calls, and meeting deadlines. Consider the exchange that took place half a century ago between Vladimir and Estragon in Samuel Beckett's *Waiting for Godot*:

Vladimir: We have kept our appointment and that's an end to that. We are not saints but we have kept our appointment. How many people can boast as much?

Estragon: Billions.

Vladimir: You think so?

Estragon: I don't know.

Vladimir: You may be right.

Being ready. At a moment in history when accelerated boot-up times and slow gardens are both offered as strategies for making the most out of life, our ability to negotiate time seems ever more crucial. My sister, my compatriot in the time-margin tutorial, tells me that being on time in small ways tunes her in to larger things. "It's about being ready," she says. "It's so inherent in human nature to procrastinate, but I feel that if I can be on time for small things, then it makes me ready and prepared when larger things happen."

Patience. The game that goes by that name is everywhere. *Patience: Games for the Fireside* was published in 1870 in Boston and offered thirty variations of the single-player card game in which a player attempts to reorder a deck by suit and rank through a series of moves from one place to another, under prescribed restrictions. Today, though renamed Solitaire, the same game comes with nearly every desktop operating system, albeit with many more complicated variations. The Absolute Patience software program offers some 430 versions of the same game, but with names like Spider, Pyramid, and Klondike. Digital cards can be customized with the motifs of exotic birds, Samurai, or French royalty; the graphics of background images can be photorealistic battle scenes or mountain lakes. Games can be played with musical accompaniment, and statistics can be scored. And certainly all these digital games are played against a clock.

I am vulnerable to the habit myself. If I can get the deck reordered on the computer monitor first thing in the morning, then I gain some hope for finding a similar series of moves to transfer words from one place to another, for coaxing ideas into alignment, or for finding a logical progression or symmetry in the sentences and paragraphs that may plague me later in the day. If you can reorder the jack of spades, the ace of hearts, the ten of clubs, then that is a start at sorting things out. Rank and color and numbers—a series of symbols is the beginning of a system with which things can be arranged. To put the cards into place requires a deliberation, a repetition of moves, an allotment of time, an attentiveness to what is right in front of your eyes, along with an appreciation for pattern, repetition, then disruption and deviation. Or maybe it is the consideration of the placement of random things and how things line up that gives the card game an almost meditative quality.

All of which makes me wonder if patience is about finding that sense of order. Perhaps it is the ability to calibrate our own experiences and thoughts, our own expectations and actions, to be in some kind of sync with what is happening around us.

The symbols and numbers on a deck of cards can be an efficient place to start—a catalog of images, numbers, and rhythms. But I also know it is possible to look to a different suite of organizing devices for patience. If it is a visual system with which to organize experience you are after, then how things in the natural world align—or sometimes do not—may offer a more comprehensive model.

I live with my husband and children in New York State's Hudson Valley, and one autumn, when my twin sons were maybe three or four, the dazzling pageantry of maple leaves in the fall was pointed out anew to me. One afternoon, just as the leaves were beginning to change their color, the boys were playing outdoors at the edge of the lawn where the grass meets the woods. All of a sudden, my son Noel ran indoors and with great astonishment announced that a light had been turned on in the woods. "Come see, come look!" he begged us, eager to share his discovery. And it was true enough. When my husband and I went outdoors, there it was, amid the locusts, birches, hemlocks, and oaks: The leaves of a small sugar maple at the edge of the woods had turned a brilliant gold and, capturing the full September light, indeed seemed to cast a radiance across the afternoon.

I have noticed that some similar switch is turned on often when one looks to nature. It can clarify things for us—even reveal us to ourselves. It is not that nature offers us metaphors for experience; rather, it demonstrates patterns of behavior, cycles of continuance, or modes of endurance that can have some tangential relevance to human experience. Nature gives us a sense of measure— though, at the same time, it may be what the writer Sherwood Anderson called "a bigness outside of ourselves." We are often more receptive to news of ourselves when it comes from some area of life distinct from the vagaries of human behavior. Often those qualities that seem so difficult for us to grasp have a way of clarifying themselves in the natural world.

Patience, a quality that comes to few of us intuitively, can be observed, imagined, possibly even learned and documented in the natural world. Possibly it is the patience that arrives through simple repetition. Or the distinction between patience for the known and patience for the unknown. Or what separates a sense of urgency from impatience. So much about how we practice patience has to do with how we experience time. What better icon for patience is there than the enduring sense of permanence the universe provides?

The natural world has a habit of knocking us into the present. And it offers a different catalog of images, numbers, rhythms—a smudge of goldenrod, or the outline of an oak leaf, or some particular arrangement of frost on a wild blackberry bush. All of these can inspire us to reflect on the placement of random things. All of these can offer lessons on being ready, whether the arc of time is minute to minute, month to month, or year to year. And at a time when life seems to happen too quickly or too slowly, a sense of order can be derived from all of these events in the natural world.

I haven't yet made any final count, nor do I know whether there are thirty variations or 430. But I do know that such events offer their own palettes, textures, and symphonies of sound, and it only follows that I have come to think of them all as my own variations of Absolute Patience.

one

Clove Meadow

When April came around last year, my husband and I made a decision about the meadow. Not that it is a meadow exactly, but a wide patch of yard out behind the house that, for years, we've kept mown. Last year, however, we revisited that choice, allowing it to grow out. Just to see, we told ourselves. It wasn't a question of whether we wanted a shorn, emerald lawn or not. Rather, it was about allowing the grass to take its own course. And waiting to see what might happen.

There was nothing especially sublime about what grew in. It was simply a catalog of ordinary northeastern weeds—clover, bluegrass, fescue, buttercups, dandelions, goldenrod, onion weed, crabgrass, wild mustard, and more that I am unable to put a name to. A smattering of wild daisies has woven itself through the ryegrass and timothy. I have heard of a weed called devil grass that has become invasive in this area, and I am curious as to whether it has taken hold here. The contrarian in me hopes for a few strands of that as well. And at dusk, when the light is just right, you can make out the cloud of insects that have taken up residence here. But all of it, the named and the unnamed, the known and the unknown, has grown in at its own particular speed, to its own particular height and reach, making, in the end, for what I have come to think of as the rough, green texture of the unexpected.

Inaction, this exercise reminds me, has value when it is attended by watchfulness. Maybe that adds up to patience. When I told my friend Greg this, he told me he thought that patience is a virtue so large it has two opposites: anger and sloth. And both, he added, incur an engagement with time that works against us: Anger is volatile, intemperate. Anger's sense of time is the time of apocalypse, the exploding of hope and of any vision of opportunity. Sloth, in all its inertia, simply negates the passage of time. Its sense of time is the time of entropy, dissolution, wastefulness.

Patience, positioned someplace on the far side of both outrage and paralysis, is the ability to move forward on imperfect information. It is agricultural, a form of farming whatever land needs cultivating. And it loves the present.

It makes sense that Greg and I had this conversation in a swimming pool. We are swimming friends, and our conversations often take place before and after we swim laps, an enterprise that is at once fluid and exact, imprecise and measured. Like other forms of meditation, it can be at once repetitive and meandering. It lends itself to both loose, associative thinking and to a precise count. You might say that swimming, itself, is an exercise in patience.

Now, when I look at this shining index of grass, weed, and wildflower, it suddenly looks to be a wide meadow, indeed. "If the single man plant himself indomitably on his instincts, and there abide, the huge world will come around to him," Ralph Waldo Emerson said in 1837, speaking to patience and all its assorted shades. But he might as well have been talking about this wild assembly of grass that is pollinated by nothing more than the wind. And when I take in this full spectrum of color, texture, the sheen of leaves and radiant blades, I am glad we took the time to wait for it.

But by midsummer it has become something else, with a denser texture. Queen Anne's lace, jewelweed, coneflower, milkweed, and sprays of chicory were thrown into the mix, now lavish, thick, nearly impenetrable. By mid-August, the sun is much lower in the sky, and in the afternoon, the diminished angle of its rays casts a violet light across the meadow. Some of the greens have faded, and the fragile texture and acid citrus of spring has been replaced by a thickness and height, and the new texture of the meadow takes on the afternoon light with dusty taupes, strands of lavender, a new golden sheen. Just as the grass and flowers seem to have braided themselves together with greater texture and density, so do they weave in the light with a deeper glow.

When I was young, my family lived in Thailand, and my mother became enchanted with the work of the Thai silk weavers. She bought yards and yards of the shimmering fabric, visited dress-makers and upholsterers, and had shirts sewn for my father, blouses and dresses for her daughters, and slipcovers, too—all in those transcendent silk stripes. Years later, when we lived in New York's Hudson Valley and some of those things had become worn, she would write letters and place orders with her old friends at the Thai silk work-shops in an attempt to replace them. And when she did that, she would give my sister and me the frayed shirt or slipcover and ask us to try to repli-cate the hues with watercolors, so that she could send a sample to the studios. And I remember staring at these stripes of olive, russet, and gold, or the large squares of lemon, ruby, and violet. My sister and I tried repeatedly, but the time, the discipline, the deliberation in trying to reproduce these graphs of color were beyond us. Trying to recreate the iridescence of those shining silk stripes and blocks of color was an elusive exer-cise that required nothing less than the ability to transcribe light.

When I look at this field of color now, I am reminded of that futile exercise. What garden could take on summer light quite the way these wild grasses do? My husband is a skilled gardener, and his carefully tended beds of tomatoes and basil, the row of blueberry bushes, the fence of climbing roses—all of these provide their own charts of sufficiency. All of them are full of their own radiant color, flavor, and texture. Yet when I take in the garden that has been fenced to keep out the deer, or the lawn of cut grass that lies nearby, the meadow, with all its texture, color, and variety, appears to be some weird acreage of possibility. And the work of the cultivated garden looks to me like the efforts of a child with a paint box trying to replicate the glow in a stripe of silk, so that a tailor half a world away will understand the color in front of her eyes.

I know there is a science to growing a meadow. Done properly, I am told, it requires clearing the ground completely, then planting a careful selection of plants and grasses that will thrive in your particular climate and soil. Seed mixes and grasses, planted in careful furrows, can be precisely choreographed for color, texture, and height. Getting the right blend and waiting for the plantings to reach maturity can take years. Nurturing the blend of fast-growing wildflowers and more slow-growing perennials relies on multiple growing seasons. But such deliberation—indeed, exercising so many choices—distracts us from the very essence of what we are after, and we prefer to follow Emerson's directive to abide and wait for the world to come around to us.

Which it does, in a blaze of wild and unprejudiced growth. Of course, I know that a sense of reason prevails here—a botanical logic governs which plants allow others to grow alongside them and which strangle off others. But no sense of discrimination presents itself to my eye. If there is a sense of order here, it is inexplicit.

Václav Havel, the former president of the Czech Republic, touched on this theme in "Planting, Watering, Waiting," a speech about the variations in waiting he came to be familiar with in a country that had waited generations for its freedom. He speaks of the kind of waiting that is without hope,

defined by silence and suppression and by the loss
of will. His own frustration as a leader, he says,
came from that conviction that transformation was
coming too slowly.

"Today, looking back," he said, "I'm beginning
to understand that I was succumbing to that sort of
impatience so destructive in modern technocratic
civilization with all its rationality, that is wrongly
persuaded that the world is nothing but a crossword puzzle in which there is only a single correct
solution to the problem; a solution I felt I alone
could find. I thought time belonged to me. This
was a great error. The world and history are ruled
by a time of their own, in which we can creatively
intervene but never achieve complete control." And
he comes to realize that "one cannot fool a plant
anymore than one can fool history. But one can
water it. Patiently, every day. With understanding,
with humility, but also with love."

"Thank you for your patience." I have said this
myself countless times and have had it said to me
hundreds, maybe thousands, of times. It is something that summons up a kind of gratitude in all
of us. But what, exactly, is that gratitude for? For
understanding, humility, and love, certainly, but

also for time, for waiting, for generosity, for forgetting, for remembering, for being attentive, and for being oblivious—for a broad spectrum of loosely affiliated sentiments, actions, and tendencies that allows things to happen.

The realization that one cannot take ownership of time seems central to the practice of human faith. "What is the value of an hour or a year when all time flows into eternity?" asks Buddhism, in which patience begins with the acceptance of pain and a transcendent tolerance. In the Buddhist kingdom of Bhutan, national well-being is measured not by GNP but by GNH, or Gross National Happiness. Its social experiment suggests that a thriving and healthy society is reflected not by economic output but by an index of happiness, which, not surprisingly, puts a high value on the unhurried life. Whether work, family, or spiritual practice, life is lived in the present moment. The Buddhist concept of mindfulness is about recognizing the reality of the moment rather than being driven by hope, fear, anticipation.

This is vastly different from the Christian view of patience, which proposes that God works through human lives and that such work is not always visible or apparent to us, nor is it completed in a single lifetime. The concept of eternal life in the Christian faith expands time into a spiritual realm. It only makes sense, then, that immortality is the mother of patience, as was suggested by John Calvin, the sixteenth-century French theologian. In Christianity, patience is more a question of accepting the mysteries of divine work, and understanding patience as such is not a source for anguish but, rather, a divine gift.

Though springing from profoundly different religious traditions, both spiritual practices recognize that the events and patterns in one's life conform to a timetable not constrained by individual experience; and that recognition, as well as the willingness to allow life to unfold in its own time, affords a certain grace.

There is something lavish about such acceptance. In August, it is not just the content of the meadow that has become extravagant, but also what occurs there. At night the deer come to sleep in the tall grass, as is evidenced by patches where the grass and wildflowers have been pressed flat, as though some torrent of water has washed across them. And often, in the morning, you will see the work of the grass spiders who have found in the stem of wild carrot and a stalk of ryegrass some structure to which to attach their silk. A thread of wild marjoram and a blade of timothy is all the framework needed to support a membrane of silk and water. This is the battalion of sheet-web weavers, but their work is visible only in the early morning, when the dew has collected across their domes and saucers and little bowls. Their entire village of tensile structures is built with thread and water—delicate and temporary constructions, but still efficient in capturing their prey.

These Frank Gehrys of the insect world weave and stretch their silver sheets, twisting, curving, swooping across the meadow in unpredictable visual rhythms. Indeed, considering the thrum of activity in the grass here, it doesn't take much to imagine these membrane structures as the miniature symphony halls, theaters, and museums of insect life. Indoors, spiderwebs usually resonate with something that is old, untouched, and forgotten—the fuss and clutter of furniture that has remained in place too long, floorboards that have never seen a broom. But when you are looking across the long grass on an August morning, this improvisational tent village speaks instead to a kind of freshness, a newness, of life happening all around you: an atmosphere of *instantaneity*.

Much continues to happen while we are doing nothing, and there is reassurance to be found in the industry of small things. Life goes on without us. It was Franz Kafka who said, "You do not need to leave your room. Remain sitting at your table and listen. Do not even listen, simply wait. Do not even wait, be quite still and solitary. The world will freely offer itself to you to be unmasked, it has no choice, it will roll in ecstasy at your feet." If these words, written by a Bohemian Jewish scholar of the absurd in 1917, can so precisely echo those of the transcendentalist pastor of the Concord School in Massachusetts some eighty years earlier, surely they speak to the universality of such counsel.

And rolling in ecstasy at my feet is just what this riot of chicory, wild garlic, and ryegrass is doing now. Maybe this is what my friend Karen means when she says, "The more you wait, the more you see." She is a garden photographer, and her professional philosophy has as much to do with planning to be lucky as with anything else. As she puts it:

My work is all about running and waiting.
I might be waiting for a cloud to shield the
sun as a way to filter the light a little, or
for the wind to subside and stop blowing
things around. And when you take that
time to wait, you start noticing things. It
can pull you in more. When you are still,
things come to you. When I'm working, it
is easy to overlook the obvious. I may be
looking at the background, or snipping a
branch that allows a view through, that
lets the eye in. And I may not notice the
mulch, the cigarette butt, the spent day lily
or the plant that needs deadheading in the
foreground. But it's not just about missing
these mundane things. It's also about getting
that transcendent flicker of light, the instant
that really makes a photograph come alive.
You have to be still to be observant enough
to know when it hits. It's easy to be so detail-
oriented that you miss the big picture.

Maybe at its best, patience has a kind of inclusiveness to it. Possibly what you are waiting for will come to pass. But so, too, will a myriad of other unexpected things. In a short reflection called "Him Who Waits," the Sufi mystic Idries Shah writes, "They say, as you know, that all things come to him who waits. We are not told, of course, what eventually happens to this well-endowed individual. But, what a prospect! Not 'what he wants comes to him who waits.' Not 'what he needs.'—But *all* things!" And maybe that is the lesson here in the meadow, that patience is not a linear exercise, but rather a practice that has multiple directions and dimensions. Real patience is likely to mandate some recognition of the unknown and the idea that anything can happen. Patience often has an object, but when it does not, a deeper sense of expectance and watchfulness can emerge.

Most of us have a tendency to wait for the wrong thing, or, at best, a questionable ability to identify what is worth waiting for. How many times have I waited for a phone call, a letter, a vacation, a job offer, only to be rewarded by what happened instead? Last June I waited for the blueberries in the garden to ripen, but it was the bumper crop of raspberries in July that surprised us most. When my son was in high school, I waited for him to improve his grade in math, but he astonished me by being elected to the Student Council instead.

In the age of multitasking, cognitive psychologists have come up with the term "inattention blindness" to describe the tendency to overlook what is happening directly in front of you because you are preoccupied with something else—the call on your iPhone, the text message, or music. But expectation can be just as distracting as these electronic devices. Not long ago, I was sitting at my desk, anticipating a call from my son at college, hoping to hear from a friend who had just started a new job, awaiting feedback from an editor reviewing a story I had written. I was so preoccupied by all of these expectations, I failed to notice my husband installing the blue jay house just yards from my window. How often do we miss what is happening in front of our eyes only because we are diverted by anticipation of something else?

As a writer, I experience this anticipatory befuddlement often. Once I traveled to Finland to interview the designers of a cell phone but found the real story in a snow castle where visitors could learn to sleep on slabs of ice. And when I imagined

I would be writing a magazine story about the architectural model for a museum, the model maker took me to the loft above his studio where he had constructed a scale model representing the star formations of the outer galaxy. The story is only sometimes where you think it is.

If you are tempted to imagine patience as a passive exercise, this is where you are likely to find yourself corrected. There is also that mystery of how patience often changes the very character of what we are being patient for—in the way, for example, the hope for treatment can eventually be transformed into acceptance of the illness, or how the thing you are looking for in your husband, your wife, or your friend may suddenly emerge in yourself, or how the hope for reconciliation can reinvent itself as an understanding of differences. And surely we have all experienced this phenomenon in speech: Wait to speak, and you will almost always find that what you have to say has changed for the better.

"All holy desires grow by delay," wrote an anonymous fourteenth-century medieval monk quoted in *The Cloud of Unknowing*. I can't speak with any certainty as to what makes desire holy, but

I know that the same growth applies to more secular enterprises.

Bruce, a psychiatrist friend of mine, tells me that good treatment is a matter of lengthy, boring stretches, that effectiveness in analysis is often a question of doing nothing. He loves Samuel Beckett—*Waiting for Godot* in particular. "But Beckett is no longer the way one feels," he sighs. "Today Vladimir and Estragon would be on their BlackBerrys." You get suspicious when you hear long, enthralling stories, one after the other, he tells me. "You wonder if they are making things up. And why they would do that. Real treatment is drudgery. Time goes on and on, and nothing happens. You kick the same stone around for a while. It can take forever. You have to wait. And people don't want to do that anymore."

Which leads me to think that there are times when patience can exist independently in the unconscious mind, or when the unconscious mind grapples with the facts, assesses them, arranges them, and rearranges them before finally presenting them to the conscious mind in a way that can be understood.

But extravagance has its own life cycle, and by late August, the fragile threads of bluegrass have lost their resilience and turned a fawn color. They flatten easily and often lie smooth to the ground. The ryegrass is still tall, but its color, too, is fading. The vibrant purple of the wild marjoram has browned, the flowery heads of the Joe Pyeweed have turned burgundy, and the stalks of timothy have become dry and stiff. The goldenrod comes into its own in mid-September with its last smudges of vivid color, confirming the change of season. Along with the sprays of pale wild aster, these blossoms are all that is left. Elsewhere, one finds nothing but some quiet cadence of fatigue.

And all of this has happened in a day. Acquisition can take a lifetime; loss arrives in an instant. Or so I am tempted to think. In reality, the changing rhythm of the days has been occurring in small increments, the daylight diminishing since June only in minutes. It takes weeks for the sunlight, water, and carbon dioxide to rearrange themselves as the plants go dormant, for the stalk of wild carrot to lose its elasticity, for the bluegrass to become brittle. But human perception is capable of profound indifference, and I have remained oblivious to all of it.

Like other forms of denial, inattention blindness has its own rewards. I have sat outside nearly every evening during the summer but it is not until early September that I look up at the sky through the black leaves and am forced to notice that, at 8:00 p.m., the sky has turned a deep, dark blue. Maybe it is nothing but retaliation, but we are as capricious toward time as it is toward us.

We have all the time in the world for some things, and not a minute to spare for others. Maybe this is what Emerson was referring to when he wrote, "Patience and patience, we shall win in the last. We must be very suspicious of the deceptions of the element of time. It takes a good bit of time to eat or to sleep, or to earn a hundred dollars, and a very little time to entertain a hope and an insight which becomes the light of our life."

Now, while the crabgrass and clover are still emerald green and carpet the ground, they lie tangled with the less elastic grasses that have given up their height and reach. A Violet Tail damselfly from the marsh across the road skitters along the lapsed stalks looking for its insect prey, but nothing else seems to be moving much. At this far end of the growing season, the convergence of the animated and the fatigued somehow underscores the exhaustion of the latter. Within a matter of days, it seems this entire vertical empire has been, if not entirely leveled, then imprecisely flattened. Every stem and stalk lies at some weird diagonal, as though none of them quite knows how to reach—or how to stop reaching—for the sun anymore. The calculations of resignation are always inexact, the angles of defeat always hesitant.

Not long ago I saw an exhibit by the British artist Cornelia Parker that examined how ordinary domestic objects can have second lives. In her piece called "Rorschach," Parker arranged for such objects as a silver platter, soup tureens, sugar bowls, and a candelabra to be flattened by a 250-ton industrial press, and then reassembled their profiles as a one-dimensional still life. Flattened but not demolished, the tableware still dazzled, reflecting all the light around it. The meadow now reminds me of the radiance of the flattened silver: The banquet has ended, but we still find patterns in what remains.

The truth of the matter is, it is nearly time to mow. Even inaction needs basic maintenance. A meadow can overgrow. Better to have cattle graze. Better to burn it down periodically. In our case, better simply to mow. And if we choose not to mow now, the undergrowth will take over, and it is no longer a grassy meadow but an impassable thicket. The reduction of grass and wildflowers serves a purpose. Already, it is only a season or two away from being the beginning of a woodland. Shearing it down will prevent the seedlings from growing into bushes, shrubs, and trees. That it may be time to mow is further confirmed by the fact that the insects have completed their life cycles; the ground-nesting birds have finished breeding. The Jungian scholar James Hollis writes of the companionability of patience and grace, an alliance that makes sense to me when I take in the meadow at its wildest and most uninhibited. Because there is a point, I know, at which patience becomes a pathology, some impenetrable tangle of indulgence, denial, and entropy.

Even patience, I see, can run out of time. Patience, too, has an end, lapsing into indolence without a moment's notice. It can be the sloth my friend Greg refers to, "a squandering of time and talent. Sloth wants to stop the clock and grow fat and slow until its world sleeps." Patience can give out from fatigue in the same way desire can exhaust itself, or in the way a piece of music played too many times becomes a sickness rather than a song, or in the way soil loses its nutrients, or a piece of metal its strength.

The cracks and fissures of metal fatigue appear when it has been through too many cycles of heating and cooling, when it has expanded and contracted too many times, when it has been flexed beyond its endurance point. These sorts of failures are not limited to steel. There are times when the tumor will not shrink, when the house cannot be rebuilt, when loss is irretrievable and absence final. There are times when someone else will not do what you want, or say what you want, or give you what you want, and when waiting any of these things out becomes a parody of perseverance. In the end, there are always those few things it is either impossible or stupid to have patience for.

But mowing is not so absolute as it sounds. It is not a sheer, uniform stubble we are after. Rather, we are advised to mow to four or six inches only, enough to cut back the woody plant material—the sprouting maples, for example—but not enough to kill off the grasses and wildflowers, which will simply reseed themselves or return as perennials. We could wait until the spring when the ground has enough moisture in it to make it safe to burn the groundcover, but that seems an extreme measure to me. Burning—if you can get the permit—will rejuvenate the meadow by eliminating the hardy weeds, and in the process allow the perennials to come back stronger. If we burn at all, though, it is likely to be on a rotation of every three or four years. But such may be the rhythm of starting anything over: The point you return to needs to be carefully and precisely calibrated. It is not so much a reduction, but rather a matter of taking some finer measure of what is needed and what is not.

We wait until the first frost to mow, which arrives in early October. Its shelf of ice, thin as it may be, still manages to support the weight of unease I can't help but feel at this time of year, as the daylight diminishes, the colors fade, and the temperature drops. By mid-morning the frost will be gone, but still, for those few early hours, even the tiniest beads of ice on a leaf or blade of ryegrass speak to the more lavish blanket of cold soon to come. My husband buys new steel blades. And the day he finally mows, though well after the first frost, is in the mid-seventies. In the old parlance, it would be called Indian Summer, but today it seems more like a freakish hot spell. By the end of the afternoon, the rows of mown grass, the severed stalks of milkweed and goldenrod, the dried blossoms all seem to be vestiges of a July afternoon.

But you'd have to look closely at this residue of summer to know what's there. It is difficult to identify the remains in their diminished state. A better way might be to run your hand across their surface so you can feel the scrabbly texture of what's been left, the stiff, brittle tufts of timothy, clumps of ragweed and crabgrass, along with the softer and silkier blades of bluegrass. The blades seem to have missed some of the clover leaf, which was smashed flat by the mower. But my untrained eye cannot make out the remnants of the daisies or asters.

And I look at this meadow, shorn, trimmed of all its excess. Although its reach is now only a matter of inches, I recognize it as a place large enough to accommodate these ambiguities of patience and all of their subtleties and nuances. Its scale is vast enough to consider patience as an endeavor that can engage us minute to minute or year to year. Inch by inch, or acre by acre, it has become its own little Serengeti.

In mid-November, you'd never notice the stubble of timothy but for the way it catches the frost. And if the sunlight manages to catch what's left in just the right way, sometimes you get a glitter of russet or of gold. It's the same with the shorn bluegrass. In a month's time, these plants are all likely to be covered by snow. I think of the time it took to grow the meadow, the time it took to notice it, the time it took to mow it down, and to start over. And I wonder whether these reflect the deceptions of time, or if, in fact, they are nothing more or less than that unpredictable rhythm of the instantaneous and the enduring.

two

Jericho Bay

The landscape I know best conveys a sense of deep resolution; its different components have come to terms with one another over the millennia. The wide river, the wetlands, the farmland, the low hills of the Hudson Valley all lead to one another with a fluid sense of passage, as though they belong to and with one another. Even the erosion of sediment into its current composition of sandstone and shale that makes up the gently rounded forms of the Catskill Mountains speaks to how the passage of time blunts the sharpest edges. Vegetation, soil, and stone have come to some kind of mutual agreement to live with one another.

No such consensus has been reached on this patch of the Maine coast. Look at nearly any part of the granite coastline, and you'll find a carnival of the unresolved, the ocean smashing into rocks that have not yet agreed to reduce themselves to sand. Even the word *coastline* seems a misnomer, for there is nothing linear here, no simple demarcation between water and land. Rather, the massive boulders of pink granite seem simply to have tumbled here, piling themselves atop and across one another in some improvisational arrangement of resistance against the fluid power of the water. The composition of the stone is such that it fractures along right-angled planes, and despite the random chaos here, the precision of these breaks suggests that disorder observes its own geometry.

My husband and I have been staying in a small cabin—unfinished white pine planks indoors, weathered gray cedar shakes outdoors—poised on the edge of a rock at the edge of the ocean. I wake to the sound of the waves, the wind, and the lobster boats going out at dawn, and on some mornings these make me think we are on the edge of all possibilities. On other mornings, however, I think of nothing but the cabin's seemingly precarious hold on the land. But even with all the ambiguity of the water-world here, there is something formidable and exact in the graphics of these giant boulders. Granite resists erosion, which is why it is such a reliable building material. Indeed, out here on this peninsula in Jericho Bay, the hard chaos of pink rock continues to hold out against the sea.

Is it a greater act of patience to build something or to take it apart? To comply or to oppose? When my husband, a cabinetmaker, is building a table or a set of shelves, it is a matter of exact measurements, joinery, and fit. His dovetails speak to the grace with which woods with varying grains and densities can find a way to accommodate one another. Recently, he repaired the crack in a friend's maple salad bowl with a cherry butterfly joint. Though it didn't take long to carve out the small piece of wood in the shape of wings, the repair was a matter of days—not hours—to secure the joint, to glue it, to wait for the glue to dry, and then to plane and sand the joint to conform to the curvature of the bowl.

His focus, when he is working on something like this, reflects what the writer Winifred Gallagher calls "attentional capacity": the way our brains can focus, on productive thoughts, on the task at hand, rather than on the desired outcome. In her book *Rapt: Attention and the Focused Life*, she suggests it is a kind of concentrated attention, rather than innate intelligence or beauty or capital, that will determine the quality of our lives. She writes, "The focused life requires not just a robust capacity for paying attention but also the discerning choice of targets that will invite the best possible experience. Much is made of the fact that human beings are the only creatures to know that we must die, but we're also the only ones to know that we must find something engaging to focus on in order to pass the time."

Patience often arrives in aggregates, in small pieces, in moments. When I was in college and planning a trip to Mexico, I tried to learn Spanish by taping scraps of paper to objects all around the apartment, so I would know the correct word for *table, window, door, plate, book*. Maybe there are times when patience is a process similar to learning a foreign language—relearning the familiar, one scrap of paper, one syllable at a time. Perhaps it is a question of accumulation, whether words in a foreign language or the mastery of a specific skill. And then, repetition. Fastening meaning onto things until we believe them to be true. Maybe this is what it means to "practice patience."

At the same time, I wonder if a similar process can be applied to unlearning things, to forgetting the names of things that you no longer have any need or desire for, one by one. I'm not referring to a table, or a plate, or a book, but rather the name of an improbable hope or an unlikely prospect. As a child you find that learning requires patience; later, you find that forgetting does as well. "The human mind is an extraordinary mechanism for forgetting," my father used to tell me. He was in his seventies then, and what he marveled at was how the brain was so capable of distilling information, constantly de-acquiring all those facts, events, and names it no longer had any need for. This, too—losing irrelevant minutiae—is a part of patience.

In Buddhism, the first step in the yoga of patience is to accept the notion that anger is an evil that diminishes control, balance, and mental acuity. Tolerance, patience, and forbearance are the middle ground on the path to love and compassion, but it is in the disassembly of anger that the process begins.

I read an account once by Doris Lessing about her ruthless dismemberment of an armchair with a saw, sharp scissors, and a claw hammer. Layer upon layer of slipcovers and upholstery, silk padding, and wood were uncovered—torn, cut, surgically removed until taking the chair apart also managed to dismantle the very idea of comfort, warmth, and accommodation. It was a kind of demolition that required care, attentiveness, patience. Throughout the process, Lessing invoked the history of the chair, the country auction where she had found it, the Devonshire farm woman she had bought it from, the cottages and apartments Lessing later furnished with it, and its final undoing—first, its thick, brown corduroy cover; beneath that, a blue, floral slipcover; under that, an orange fabric with a jazz pattern; beneath that, gray sateen with tiny flowers; and finally, a layer of pink silk.

How things come apart, how they can be dismantled, or how they disintegrate on their own is a method and a process. Waves break on the shore some eight thousand times each day. I have read that, on average, 166 million tons of dissolved salts are contained in a single cubic mile of sea water—each one a vital mineral, each one its own particle of abrasion. And here, at what is called the intertidal zone, each one seems to have done its work deliberately and precisely.

This is where the tide varies from ten to twelve feet, and whatever lies in that space is submerged at high tide, exposed to the air at low tide. The zone closest to the sea—the barnacle zone—has a rough, scraggy texture of sharp shells, brittle and calcified. This is where the ocean stitches the greatest evidence of its constant arrival and retreat, where periwinkle and purple mussel shells attach themselves to the blocks of granite tumbled along the shoreline, where the tangle of rockweed can't help but grab on as well, and where the rocks are shining with water, salt, and the possibility of whatever the sea brings in.

Above the barnacle zone is the black zone—scuffed where the high tide reaches and then withdraws twice daily, and named for the blue-green algae that covers its surface and darkens over time. And above that is the spray zone, untouched by the tides themselves but sprayed continually by the waves. "It is a transitional zone," I later read in a guidebook, "neither truly marine nor terrestrial, and any organism that lives in it must tolerate both extreme desiccation and the impact of salt, wind, and surf."

Yet, observed more closely, the improvised graphics of the intertidal zone also spell out something about the way patience, tolerance, and endurance are separated by the smallest of degrees. Or maybe it is just that patience is one of our more imprecise endeavors. Yellow-and-gray lichens attach themselves here, along with a handful of sea spiders and ants. Seaside goldenrod and salt spray rose sometimes endure here as well. This is a place where the infinitesimal can grab hold.

It's easy to read the intertidal zone as some marine equivalent to the repetition that can be a force in our own lives. I remember visiting an installation of the painter Sol LeWitt just days before it opened. A room with white walls had been marked into a precise grid of large squares, inside of which were smaller squares, and inside each of these was a pattern of lines—horizontal, vertical, diagonal—no more than a quarter inch apart. Assistants, perched on rickety scaffolding, their eyes rimmed in red and their muscles slack with fatigue, were filling in these squares with the lines, drawing one after another, after another, with graphite pencils and a straight edge. It was an act of exhaustive repetition, transforming the room into a luminescent cloud of grids. It was also proof of the dazzling geometries that can emerge when we learn something simply by doing it over and over again.

The day before we leave the Maine coast, my husband and I take a walk out to Barred Island, a dot of land that can only be reached at low tide. A path through a scrub forest of spruce and hemlock, beach roses, mosses, ferns, and wild cranberries and blueberries takes us to the edge of the rocks. Inevitably, it is the wild horticulture of the ocean that draws us in the most, where the tide washes in, leaving its random tapestry, the bloated, green sacs of the bladder wrack braided with the brown, flatter strands of this ubiquitous rockweed. Against all odds, as they align themselves on the shore, the textile arts of the ocean weeds suggest that some occasional order can be made here. The sandbar connecting the island to the mainland is submerged when the tide is in, but this afternoon we have time to cross it. This is a place where, twice daily, land becomes water, and water becomes land.

An island is defined simply as any piece of land totally surrounded by the sea at mean high tide, a piece of information that easily loses meaning once you spend any time on this coastline, where the sea, sand, and rock are more intent on proving how fugitive their borders remain. Still, there is something reassuring in seeing how a place of such absolutes can also be so elusive. "The boundary between sea and land is the most fleeting and transitory feature of the earth," Rachel Carson wrote in *The Sea Around Us*, and it is oddly comforting to find that these granite coves and islands are capable of such transience.

As we sit on the slabs of granite of the island watching the tide wash into the sandbar connecting it to the mainland, another family arrives with picnic baskets. The boy, called Pablo, does what most young boys would do. He kicks around the sand, he grabs a stone and throws it into the sea, he collects a handful of purple mussel shells, he wades into the shallow water, he walks back and forth across the narrowing bar. And suddenly, then, he understands. In the same way my own son years earlier had been witness to the shine of a sugar maple on an October afternoon, he understands how some small rhythm of nature can sometimes align itself, for a moment, with that of ordinary human experience. Though it is a configuration of sand rather than leaves, some similar switch has been turned on.

Pablo looks to one side and then to the other. There are two beaches here—two places where the water washes in. And, delirious with joy, he begins to run from one beach to the other, a matter of about twenty feet. But that distance is enough. Perhaps as an adult he will understand the marine science that explains the fugitive borders of sea and land, but for now it is enough to mark that place with his own footsteps. Back and forth he runs, each time examining his position and what the last small wave has delivered, as though the incoming tide of one beach might offer something more than that of the other, some different arrangement of rock, shell, and weed. Perhaps, even, the seawater on one beach is preferable to the seawater found at the other.

And all the while his mother is watching him. She has half an eye to the waves, while attending to another, smaller child in that way that a mother of young children is able to intuit what is happening around her. It occurs to me that patience comes more easily to women. Academic research studies from the 1970s, when women's sports were challenging many popular assumptions about their athletic skills, found that women are particularly adept at many forms of endurance—that sibling of patience—whether it be an ease at acclimatization or the ability to take in oxygen during strenuous exertion. But surely it is not the running of marathons or open water distance swimming that reflects women's capacity for endurance, but rather the cycle of pregnancy and childbirth that familiarizes them with notions of anticipation and inevitability.

I remember trying to carve up the giant patience that seemed required of me when I was waiting for the unfathomable—the birth of my own twin boys. Perhaps it could be broken up, I thought, into smaller, more manageable increments. If I could pull off waiting gracefully, say, for the tomatoes in the garden to ripen, for the peonies to bloom, for my husband to build shelves in what would be the boys' room, then perhaps I could pull off waiting for nine months.

And so I waited for the peonies in June, for a manuscript to be published, for my husband to build the shelves, and for all the countless other small events that require our minor feats of perseverance. And I did so with a complete lack of grace. Human understanding of any sort had vanished. I barely enjoyed the bloom of the peonies when they finally arrived, was careless with the manuscript, thankless toward my husband. Waiting for the water to boil, I would be out of sorts, and the line at the grocery store was a justifiable cause for fury. But I felt no sense of urgency for the larger event, which, oddly enough, seemed manageable. Perhaps the lesson is that our behavior rarely observes a sense of measure—we can fail at small tasks and still succeed at the larger ones.

This predicament is not peculiar to apprehensive pregnant women. A friend of mine in the publishing industry has no difficulty waiting eighteen months for a book to come out, but the five minutes spent waiting for a bagel at the local deli irritates him no end. In his book, *Faster*, an examination on the acceleration of modern culture, James Gleick speaks of the shared assumption among prison inmates that a short-term sentence is more difficult to live with than a long-term sentence. It is "the difference between waiting and living," he suggests. And he notes that, after being released from the gulag, Alexander Solzhenitsyn found himself more bored during the sixteen minutes spent waiting for the trolley than he had ever been during his empty sixteen-hour days while imprisoned.

I like to think that most of us have some inner timepiece that parses out our tolerance, but perhaps, in a culture of acceleration, this timepiece is in overdrive. At a time when instant communication provokes us to feel tremendous urgency about the most mundane things, I would hope for some interior balance sheet that enables us to wait for others. But my suspicion is that, if such a balance sheet exists at all, it is not any orderly presentation of data—there is no chance of finding a carefully structured chart with tidy rows and columns and exact measures. Rather, it is some haphazard scribbling, some improvisational and less-inhibited form of bookkeeping with wild leaps of hope and incomprehensible lapses of logic. This impressionistic memorandum that reflects on how we give time to some things and not to others likely has mostly to do with the anarchy that attends human desire.

The memo might look something like the drawings my friend Barbara Flanagan does when she is in her car. She calls them "Driving Drawings": "The trick is to draw without looking at the paper, and to change pens, pencils, and colors without taking my eyes off the road." With quick short strokes or with longer swooping curved lines, she fills sheets of blank paper with squiggles, marks, and curlicues—whole clouds of color take shape during the time it takes her to move her son to his college dorm in a slow rental truck, to drive to visit her mother, to drive to a funeral in Princeton. Such sketches, she says, take an amazing amount of time, mileage, and pigment. "I don't know," she told me once. "It's as though there is some kind of chemical in my brain, and when I start drawing, I feel ready to respond to anything that happens on the road. And it's also about having something to show for all those miles of driving."

These drawings document something about how hope and stamina can be imprinted on each other, layer, upon layer, upon layer, to make a composition of their own, but they also read to me as some kind of manifesto on patience, some kind of human equivalent to the fretwork the ocean leaves on the granite.

"As soon as I start drawing," Barbara says, "my senses seem to wake up and get coordinated, making me watch the road and work the controls with a more gentle, focused kind of concentration." Maybe it is just a question of being attentive to some unseen rhythm of expectation, to some accidental pattern or observation of time. But I think that in the same way that a random arrangement of curious squiggles can eventually become a vermilion cloud, or that some dense crosshatching of quick strokes finally morphs into a rolling green field, maybe patience is, at the best of times, something we arrive at when we are doing something else.

Change, after all, arrives on its own timetable. Maybe the most we can do is honor a sense of imminence. Consider the words of Argentine writer Jorge Luis Borges: "Music, states of happiness, mythology, faces molded by time, certain twilights and certain places—all these are trying to tell us something, or have told us something we should not have missed, or are about to tell us something; this imminence of a revelation that is not yet produced is, perhaps, the aesthetic reality." Patience allows for this sense of imminence.

Pablo's mother, still waiting for him, evokes an icon of patience: another woman by another ocean—Odysseus's wife, Penelope—weaving at her loom by day and undoing the work by night as she awaited her husband's return. It's a portrait of patience that implies a kind of control, as well as the suggestion that patience can sometimes be a matter of both doing and undoing, fastening and unfastening, stitching and unstitching. Maybe these are parallel skills: the tenacity it takes to construct something, to make a meal, to learn a language, to build a boat, and the discipline required to take something apart, to undo a season, to forget a year, to disassemble an expectation. Perhaps patience, by necessity, weaves remembering with forgetting, a methodical process of going forward and going back. Perhaps patience is compliance and resistance, a way of knowing something and not knowing it, too, where the known and unknown are threaded together.

And it occurs to me, then, that there are two kinds of patience—for the known and for the unknown. On the first, it is possible to fasten desire and expectation. In it lies that quiet, abiding trust that what you are waiting for will arrive in its time, that inevitability has its own cycles and rhythms. Possibly it is akin to this human compulsion of looking for order—the angles at which granite cracks or the texture and pattern with which seaweed can braid itself.

On the other hand, to have patience for something you cannot yet identify may require a wider and broader kind of trust. In exercising patience for the unknown, you find an intimacy with the impossible. What you know to be sand will suddenly become water, and when you are counting on a current you will find a beach strewn with shells, and you'll be left to intuit all that can never be. Whether the rough skin of a sand dollar or the silky iridescence of a conch, you'll run your hands across its surface and memorize the colors and the contours of all those things that will never happen.

It is likely that patience requires these two very different kinds of imagination, because in the end, of course, it is the random and unpredictable rhythm between these two that makes up the real texture and character of patience. And I think of one and then the other, not unlike the way Pablo spent the better part of one July afternoon, dashing back and forth across the narrowing sandbar, wondering with exhilaration which tide and which wave might bring him what he most desired.

three

Beacon Mountain

The switchback trail up Beacon Mountain threads its way through a forest of maple, hemlock, and oak, interrupted from time to time by thickets of thin white birches, and sometimes even by entire groves of black birch, their trunks etched with silver hieroglyphs. Laddered with roots, the path is carved by stone and strewn with rocks and gravel. Where the slope levels off, a bed of ferns has taken root. Every rift in the granite offers its own still life—a pocket of citrus-colored moss, or a handful of wild grass. A tiny, orange spider negotiates its way across both of these; a red eft scurries across an oak leaf in its own vignette of determination.

Though this winding switchback is the steady and measured route, it is interrupted from time to time with the alternative paths suggested by the geology of the mountain. Slabs of granite, gullies formed by stones washed down during spring rains, and wider trenches carved through the rocks and moss by melting snow all intersect the trail at unpredictable intervals with their own sense of frantic descent, as loose stones skitter below your feet.

If the switchback trail and these more improvisational paths forged by stone and water transcribe some diagram of purpose across the face of this mountain, the incline trail is the most direct route. It was cleared in 1901 for the construction of a railway to take visitors to the summit, and old postcards attest to a casino, an amusement park, and a dance hall built there in the early twentieth century. The gaming tables, the striped tents, and the building materials for the hotel were all hauled up the mountain by a cable car designed and installed by the Otis Elevator Company. A century later, the hotel and cottages at the summit are long gone, but the straight path neatly bisecting the face of the mountain still appears as a rude scar. The nine-hundred-foot ascent in less than half a mile is brazenly vertical. Now overgrown, thick with shrubs, only the vestige of a previous generation's hurry remains.

What is it that makes us rush toward things? Intuitively we *know* better. We *must*. The capacity for delay is a skill essential to human happiness. Our ability to postpone gratification, to not have the second or third helping, to not speak in anger, to take the time to master the skill to get the job—all of these capabilities keep us on track. The neuroscience that connects the dots between intelligence and self-control confirms that this ability to *simply wait* can be a predictor of a productive and satisfying adult life, whether it is measured in professional achievements, the ability to sustain relationships, or the foresight in planning retirement.

Social psychologist Walter Mischel's research on children and self-gratification indicates that a child's capacity to recognize the value of the deferred reward is a recognizable signal for a well-adjusted adulthood. His fabled "marshmallow" experiments—in which a group of four-year-olds were given a marshmallow and promised another if they could wait for twenty minutes before eating the first one—speak to the behavioral advantages of those capable of practicing impulse control. Tracking the children as they became adults, Mischel found that those who had been capable of waiting were more grounded and dependable adults, in addition to being emotionally intelligent.

But surely we don't need to be told this. Surely we learn as children that the rewards meted out later may have more meaning than the more immediate ones. Surely we have some intuitive knowledge that whatever stability we may have in our lives has some association with restraint.

Today, the reward of the switchback is the light that casts a glaze across the summit. The woods have thinned to a few weedy locust trees, some spindly birches, and a scattering of low sumacs. But the dwindling vegetation has been made up for by the brightness that spills through it. As part of the Hudson Highland range, Beacon Mountain marks that place where the Appalachian chain is breached by water—glaciers during the last ice age forced a rupture through the hills, and today the Hudson River streams through the highlands more as a fjord than a river. At the northern edge of these highlands, the mountain stood as a fortress and was subsequently named for its role in the American Revolution, when flares were lit at the summit to alert local militias to the advent of British soldiers on the Hudson River below.

On this September afternoon, the river is a wide shine of silver ribbon, but whether it is taking in the light or throwing it back is open to question. Not that it matters. Be it in the easy drift of a sloop skirting its surface, the speed of the Amtrak train on the eastern shore, or simply the swooping of the gulls, the fading minutes of daylight out on the river are a fluid time. Maybe it's nothing more than the rock-solid quiet of the granite mountaintop, but I am suddenly aware of the river's shifting color, its current, the gust of wind that catches a sail. The river is a place where nothing ever stops moving. But maybe any mountain at the edge of a river could tell you as much: Some things never change, other things always do, and the trick is being able to tell the one from the other.

When I had been here a few weeks earlier, a cloud bank had settled in that late summer morning, and though I had waited for the sky to clear, the river remained out of view. Offering me only sound with which to situate myself—the distant groaning of the semis on the interstate as they downshifted, or the whistle of the freight trains coursing up the west side of the river—that morning on the mountain had seemed an archive of the indefinite world.

Patience is, by nature, braided together with doubt. It demands a tolerance for ambiguity. That day, the components of uncertainty were nothing more than water particles, air, and light, but these were enough for the fog to unfurl itself over the river. Obscurity, at once comforting and bewildering, offers a wide view of the unseen and the unknown. At times settling comfortably below me as some remote vapor, leaving me a realm of light and cobalt sky, then wrapping its beads of water around me, the composition of the cloud shifted constantly—a reminder that the shape of what you do not know can change before your eyes.

I imagine my predecessors in the casino here, the uncertainty of their gambling excursions underscored by a summit trimmed in fog. What better place to guess at numbers, to make random choices, to forge an association with chance? In her poem "Turtle," Kay Ryan writes how that creature "lives below luck level, never imagining some lottery/ will change her load of pottery to wings./ Her only levity is patience,/ the sport of truly chastened things."

Surely it was the point of the cable car to assist the mountain's visitors in climbing above luck level.

Maybe patience is nothing more than a matter of having some reliable method of counting, some interior calculator that can tally up the increments of time, hope, expectation, and enterprise to come up with an equation that is clearly presented and intuitively grasped. Researchers have determined that most of us tend to underestimate the passage of time, like the famed French scientist Michel Siffre who spent two months in an underground cave living without external cues about time. Contacted by his above-ground colleagues after that time had passed, Siffre was certain only twenty-eight days had passed. Yet important events and the memory of them can work to readjust the internal clock, giving the brain something to latch on to, enabling us to parse time into segments, thus expanding it. Which is to say, how human beings calibrate their behavior with the passage of time defies logic and planning. It is an exercise at once personal, volatile, and given to whim. We are given fingers and toes to count on, but these rudimentary tools are inadequate for the calculation of time.

If you are measuring the herbs, counting the cups of broth, and adjusting the flame when you are making soup for your children, that is one kind of equation. If you are counting the years and months in an estimate of time and enterprise, that is another kind of equation. And if you are collecting the words to anything of any importance, the truth is that there can be too few words or too many words, and that determining the correct number of words is yet another equation. Patience, suggested the writer Ambrose Bierce, is a minor form of despair disguised as a virtue, but it's my bet that his count was just off, that he had miscalculated something somewhere along the line.

But we all keep count differently. I know that I keep count too precisely, too compulsively. Because the idea of the time margin was so central to my upbringing, I tend to be prompt. Invite me to dine at 7, and I will be there at 7:00 p.m.—7:05 p.m., at the latest. There is no room in my life—or so I believe—to be late for dinner or to run for a train. It is a tenacity in keeping count, a fanaticism about the minutes and hours I try to lose. I try to shake the conviction that being on time matters. What is the compulsion to be on time about? In part, it has to do with that inner clock: If I am late for dinner, then I'll wake up late the next morning, and then I will be running behind in the work I mean to do, all of which is sure to cause me to lose my step, to fall behind life's grand schedule in some essential way. Being on time can provide a sense of accommodation and order, as though one's own interior sense of time can somehow be calibrated with that of the external world.

But it also may come from an almost primal fear of missing something—a word, a conversation, an exchange, a chance to see something, find something, learn something, some opportunity that may never come again. My husband, along with every roommate I ever had before he came along, knows about my inclination to take clothes out of the dryer while they are still damp. Why wait? It's time to get on to the next thing. *That* is sure to be more interesting. It's not that I don't think there is enough time. It's just that I am certain what's next is better, more, greater. Lewis Carroll's irritable white rabbit, though glancing at his pocket watch and grumbling "Oh dear, oh dear, I shall be too late," did, after all, have an appointment with wonderland, a garden with a rose tree, kings and queens in the shape of playing cards, and a croquet game with flamingo mallets.

My talent for impatience has been rewarded by a child who has all the time in the world. My son, Luc, has a sense of time that drifts and flows. When we are trying to leave the house, when I am standing at the door with my coat on and my hand on the knob, there is always some final thing for him to do, find, get—a sweater, a wallet, a hat, a light to turn off, a door to close, a last quick phone call to make. When I am not being impatient with him, which is usually, I try to use this time to remind myself that he conforms to a different timetable. And that in our haste to get out the door, the red hat he is rushing upstairs to find is a way of saying, "I'm here, too. Notice me."

And yet, he has no time to listen to phone messages. I could not understand this until it was explained to me that it takes far less time to read a text message than it does to listen to a spoken message, that texting is *fifteen to twenty* times faster than listening to voicemail. He and his friends share the assumption that, in the age of instant information, listening to messages takes too much time. When voice-to-text services are available, the process will be hastened even more.

Which demands the question: What is the thin line that separates impatience from urgency, that combination of necessity and certainty, that imperative needed to say or do the right thing at the right time? What is the difference between racing toward something with a sense of conviction, or need, or desire, and simply rushing recklessly and impulsively? Impatience, with its multiple personalities, has an ingenuity of its own. It can come disguised as anticipation or pretend to be hope. In the beginning, wrote the nineteenth-century philosopher Søren Kierkegaard, one scarcely even recognizes it: "It is so gentle, so inviting, so encouraging, so wistful, so sympathetic—and when it has exhausted all its arts, it finally becomes loudmouthed, defiant, and wants to explain every-thing although it never understood a thing."

Maybe all that separates impatience from urgency is some kind of unblinking self-knowledge, some essential awareness of what is worth attending to. In *Rapt*, Winifred Gallagher writes:

> *Deciding what to pay attention to for this hour, day, week, or year, much less a lifetime, is a peculiarly human predicament, and your quality of life largely depends on how you handle it. Moses got his focus from God, and Picasso from his nearly supernatural creativity. We have other motivations and gifts, and most of us have to go through a more complicated process to find the right thing to focus on.*

It is not only people that conform to different calendars; events and objects do, too. A full year passed between the August morning I swam across the Hudson River and the morning I swam across the Connecticut River, and in the years following I swam other rivers—the Delaware, the Susquehanna, the Monongahela—but it wasn't until later that I understood that whatever sense of restoration I found by swimming these rivers mirrored the restoration of the rivers themselves. And then I decided this premise was full enough for a book that took years to write.

Yet when my husband and I got out of our cars in a snowstorm and walked into a small wood-frame farmhouse on a country road in the Hudson Valley in 1987—on the very first day of our search for a place to live—there was something about the stone steps, the transom light over the front door, the worn chestnut floorboards that instilled in me the conviction that we could live in this house. We made an offer on the house the next morning, closed on it a couple of months later, and have lived in it ever since.

How we live depends almost entirely upon how we measure, estimate, and otherwise arrange the distance between ourselves and everything that lives around us, at times diminishing it to the slimmest possible margin and at other times vastly and inexplicably magnifying it. What sets human beings apart from other species has been studied, recorded, and catalogued—the opposable thumb, say, or the moral compass, language with syntax, culture—but it occurs to me now that we might add to that list the imagination we use to measure time in such varied ways.

If keeping count is something we all manage to do in cycles and rhythms of our own making, small wonder that there are also times when we imagine that all of these numbers, equations, and chronologies can be tossed to chance, as the roulette wheels and gaming casino on the edge of this mountain once attested.

What's left of the hotel and casinos are now only a few overgrown pathways, cracked concrete platforms, a grove of elm trees, some old stone walls, a few chunks of concrete steps. A slab of the old foundation jammed up against the granite ledge is crumbling, and together they exhibit the varied composites of hardness and resistance piled up next to each other. This afternoon on the summit, the remains of gaiety are simply a monarch butterfly, an abrupt stand of goldenrod, and the sound of wind rippling through the leaves of an aspen tree.

The crumbling remains of the brick power-house read as a graph of decay. Each facade is made up of three walls of brick stacked up right next to the other, and each is disintegrating at its own particular rate. Inside, ferns and sumac bloom over the giant, rusting wheels and pulleys that once hauled the cable cars up the mountain, and its system of cogs and weights has been threaded with wild asters and purple clover. A random calligraphy of graffiti and wild ivy—that universal language of abandoned places—streams across the bricks themselves, which are now turning to powder while flakes of rust adorn the machinery.

Now, considering the amusement park once poised on this arid ledge of the earth's crust, I wonder at our abiding instinct to bring a sense of spontaneity to those places where it seems to least belong. Surely, among our transactions with the natural world, this is the most inexplicable— odder than insisting that we can climb an icy cliff or maneuver a kayak down a thundering river is that impulse to bring a sense of play where it is most out of place. But it is probably more than the contrarian in us. For all its lightheartedness, play can be a driving force in endurance.

In *Rapt*, Gallagher suggests that there are times in which play—that is, turning work into a game, a rote activity into something that engages the imagination—can be a way of focusing attention on the present moment. High achievers, she suggests, have this ability to construct little puzzles for themselves. Thomas Jefferson, when not occupied "with the demands of the Revolution or the presidency, for example, delighted in making and designing simple, useful things, such as keys and a plow."

And, certainly, such play does well to occupy the mind in times of duress. Sometimes patience is simply a form of distraction, or what the ceramic artist Eva Zeisel calls "thought control." Imprisoned by Joseph Stalin in 1936 for sixteen months, twelve of which were spent in solitary confinement, Zeisel did not allow herself to remember the past or dream of the future. Instead, she designed a brassiere, did headstands riding an imaginary bicycle in the air, and played chess games with herself on a fantasy board.

I have encountered this intersection of patience and play before. During the time our family lived in Thailand, I contracted tuberculosis, and the infection in my lungs sometimes prevented me from playing with my friends outdoors. On such afternoons, I would sit on the veranda with my nurse—a young, widowed Japanese woman who had come to our family in Bangkok after the war, leaving her own teenage children behind in Japan. We would sit together at a table, and she would teach me how to fold brightly colored squares of paper into all manners of boats, flowers, horses, birds, and cranes.

It wasn't until decades later, when I was a mother myself, that I came to wonder about those afternoons. I don't know whether she was rapt or practicing thought control, but I think it's possible that folding and creasing and rearranging those squares of paper into their fantastic shapes was not only a way for her to cheer up a sick child, but also a way—through a combination of discipline, vivid imagination, and tactile ingenuity—to bring every part of her being to accommodate those ways in which her own life had been so unexpectedly rearranged, to use distraction to survive her separation from her family.

Now, that impulse to sit in a room trying to make one thing become another, not with a piece of bright paper but with a word or a sentence, may spring from those afternoons on that wide veranda overlooking the lily pond, banana and mango trees, a wandering water buffalo or, possibly, a Buddhist monk in his saffron robe. When I think of the magic with which she could string together a chain of shining birds, boats, and flowers, I realize how very little separates play from distraction, and how little difference there is between distraction and patience. It is natural to use play to stay with something we would be unable or unwilling to stay with otherwise, because it is possible for play to overlap with the repetition, discipline, and stamina required to solve a puzzle or to turn a square of colored paper into a crimson peony, a jade crane, or a turquoise rowboat.

Which, in turn, distracts us from the past and the future.

Standing in the remains of the powerhouse, I look at what's left of the old machinery. I know it is a matter of steel cables and pulleys, but when I think of those old photographs of crowds coming up the mountain, I wonder if it isn't really the sheer weight of their commitment to play that is pulling them up the incline.

I also wonder who practiced their enterprise with the greater sense of urgency: the militia members lighting their signal fires to convey the imminent threat of military invasion, or the couples in the cable cars determined to drink champagne and dance the foxtrot at the mountaintop pavilion. It is clear to me now that beauty contests and roulette wheels probably belonged up here just as surely as the flares a century and a half earlier. If you are looking for the news that everything is about to be upended, you have every reason to want to receive it from a mountain that is rock solid.

I encountered an elderly man I had passed earlier on the trail, who told me he had emphysema. "I think I spent as much time on my way up waiting as I did walking," he said. Then he gestured at the view—the distant ridge of the Catskill Mountains, a barge drifting along the wide river that flows miles below us to the west, and the grove of trees we are standing under now—and sighed with exasperation. "I feel like a fool not knowing what these trees are," he said. But I suspect there was another reason he felt foolish. In the sensation of altitude is the suggestion that we can be lifted out of ourselves. It is the logical outcome of any quest for high ground to feel diminished, as it is sure to confound whatever interior sense of measure we may have devised for ourselves.

Imagining his labored steps up the trail, I wonder if they spell out something about the difference between the patience that is imposed upon us and the patience that we practice deliberately, between the circumstances that impose a sense of measure and delay on our lives and our own active hesitation or dogged waiting. And suddenly these choices seem too limited, and I know that what I am after is the trick of spontaneous waiting, the kind of patience that can be turned on and off with ease. Maybe it requires nothing more than the knack for being recklessly patient. This requires, of course, an unlikely lineup of human impulse and ability, well above my own luck level. But then who could blame me for trying? I am not the first person to come up this mountain on a gamble, hoping it's my lucky day.

four

The East Woods

Before long, leaf by leaf, the woods begin to lose their color. Wild blackberries, brambles, goldenrod fade. The locust trees, black oaks, hickories, and maples are drained of their radiance one by one. The Indian grass, wild rye, and jewelweed wither. When the snow comes, it almost always comes from the west, in clouds so weighed down it is hard to believe what falls from them arrives with such lightness. Only the eastern pines retain their blackish-green hue, and the first flurries in November settle on the land to affix some gentle but final stamp confirming that the color has officially leached out of the landscape.

In winter, it is again possible to learn how the distance between things defines them. That space between the trees is how you come to know them—to become familiar with the bones of the landscape, the skeletal overlay of the canopy, the calligraphy of branches and vines.

In a drawing class I took in high school, much of the curriculum had to do with exercises in attention. To develop an awareness of space, we were advised to draw trees. "Use all the graphic possibilities of weight, tone, value, and texture and line quality to convey a stand of trees," the textbook instructed. "These will signal what is distant and what is close."

Now, against the backdrop of snow, the indecisiveness of the pin oak in the foreground is clear: Its lower branches droop to the ground, while the branches near the top of the tree reach upward. The smooth skin of a yellow birch and the irregular, curling strips that seem to crack and peel off the trunk of a shagbark hickory behind it are suddenly made visible by the whiteness around them. If there are graphic possibilities presented in these trunks and all their tracery, it has everything to do with the full-board length of winter.

In the same way that the trees become more visible against the white screen of the snow, it is often the time before and after that articulates experience. "Wait as long as you need to," writes Lynne Cox in her 2006 memoir, *Grayson*. "The waiting is as important as the doing." Cox knows something about patience. *Grayson* describes a long-distance swim in the Pacific Ocean off the coast of Long Beach, California, more than thirty years ago when Cox, then 17, encountered an orphan baby whale on her return to shore. She describes the changing currents and the riptides she found herself caught in as she attempted to reunite the whale with its mother and recalls swimming alongside bat rays, past the clusters of moon jellies, amid a school of sunfish. Waiting for the whale's mother to appear transformed a routine training session into a life-altering ocean passage, and in the decades following that morning swim, she finds herself imagining the whale, now an adult, full of power and strength and song. And crafting out of that encounter a theory on the purpose of the "in between," she writes:

It's the time you spend training and the
rest in between. It's painting the subject
and the space in between; it's the reading
and thinking about what you've read; it's
the written words, what is said, what is left
unsaid, the space between the thoughts on the
page, that makes the story, and it's the space
between the notes, the intervals between fast
and slow, that makes the music. It's the love
of being together, the spacing, the tension of
being apart, that brings you back together.
Just wait. Just be patient, he will return.

In the age of speed-dial phones and one-minute bedtime stories, Cox's meditation on patience seems of another time. It also offers a poignant message to an oversaturated, accelerated world: Absence—of things, of people, even of baby whales—amplifies shape. The sphere of time around an event shapes our experience of it. Time is a magnifying glass: To wait for something expands it in the same way that remembering something often makes it larger.

Sitting on the mantel over the fireplace in the dining room is an antique clock that belonged to my grandfather. The elegant clock face is encircled in brass and inset in a sturdy alabaster column about eight inches high, and there is something in the milky veins of the stone that underscores the delicacy of the Roman numerals on the clock face. When it came into my possession, the old clock was broken, and after much research my husband and I found a man to repair it. He was elderly, and when we drove from our Hudson Valley home to visit him in the Connecticut barn where he had set up shop, it seemed appropriate that our route took us across an eighteenth-century covered bridge. Inside his shop was all manner of antique clocks: a bronze figural clock with the huntress Diana draped over the face, vintage porcelain clocks bedecked with garlands of roses, nautical clocks designed to roll with the waves—all of it an archive of the ingenuity, mechanical and decorative, that we have brought to the practice of telling time.

My husband and I knew that repair was a matter of cleaning and replacing parts of the clock's inner workings, yet something in the way the repairman ran his hands over the alabaster contours made us think it was a question of healing as well. A month or so later, when we went to pick it up, he explained that he had rebalanced the pendulum. To function properly now, the clock would need to rest on a perfectly level surface.

Once home, we carefully positioned the clock on the mantle. It reliably told us the time for about two hours.

We knew that the problem was a matter of balance, but much as we tried to level the heavy stone properly with a series of paper-thin wooden shims, it was impossible to get it quite right. As a cabinetmaker, my husband understands the precision needed to measure and produce a level surface. He does this, I would say, nearly every day of his life. But there was something about this mantel, in this room, in this old house, where nothing is ever plumb, where there are few straight lines, clean edges, or level planes. So, for nearly twenty years now, the time displayed on that mantel has been 9:06.

Though it is incapable of telling us the hour of day, the alabaster clock conveys a different and equally precise message about time. Over the years, in a house full of timepieces—a stove and coffeepot that state the minutes in blinking LED displays, a wristwatch, a chirping alarm clock, cell phone screens—I have found it useful to have this one, static clock. The clock on the mantel reminds me that while attending to the seconds and minutes and hours is important, no less so is understanding how a disruption of interior weights and balances can arrest time altogether. "Patience is always just as active as it is passive and just as passive as it is active," said Kierkegaard. And while all the other timepieces in my house seem to be moving toward some destination or other—counting down to a meal, an arrival, a departure, a pill to take, a call to make—I think of the clock on the mantel as an instrument that confirms appointments with hope, trust, curiosity, tolerance, endurance, and an entire range of anticipatory sensations.

I would guess that most of us could use more practice, not only in the passive variety of patience, but in the active attentiveness to the rhythm of things—the interplay between the passive and the active, to know when time stops and when it has managed to pick up again. "When you do some-thing," my friend Janet says, "or say something to someone, in conversation or in interaction, things have their own rhythm, and often you have to wait to know what it is, or to let it play out."

Perhaps what Janet is talking about is no dif-ferent than the arrangement of words in a poem, where indentations and line breaks suggest weight, a pause, or some greater lapse of time. But I think she is also saying something about how patience inhabits the present. And it occurs to me that this is the great paradox of patience: It is concerned wholly with time, and yet has nothing to do with it. It is predicated on there being a future, and yet it insists that we be rooted in the present. Or, to put it another way: Patience may not be a virtue so much as an experience that demands both a passionate engagement with time and a complete indifference toward it.

Perhaps the stillness inside patience can be looked upon as a frame for experience, because *how* we wait for something, *how* we expect an event to occur, colors how it comes to be. Perhaps the surround is a baroque Venetian gilt frame carved with ornate medallions and roses and cascading leaves, or possibly a painted wood frame with lapis and ebony inlays. Or it might be a French gothic frame with architectural motifs—possibly a small city of churches or a crown of miniature cathedrals piled up on one another like so many small prayers and promises and appeals full of urgency and apprehension, like those that embellished each moment of the evening that I waited for my teenage son to arrive home safely from Vermont during a snowstorm.

Had I been the one driving, the snow on the windshield, the slick of ice on the road, the needle on the speedometer would have required a different brand of attentiveness, and it might have been a simple black walnut frame with a precisely inscribed geometric motif spelling out measure and deliberation. But I remember, too, a photograph of a frame that had been sculpted as the outline of a monstrous mask—the face of a writhing creature from the ocean, its gaping mouth the aperture for some small painting or drawing. Which certainly can describe the tormented kind of patience, resonant with uncertainty, that is required to wait for illness to take its course, to settle in, or to retreat.

In her essay "Waiting," the Irish writer Edna O'Brien catalogues the many varieties of waiting: "There is the angry waiting, the plaintive waiting, the almost cheerful waiting in which we believe for certain that the phone call or revelation will occur presently." Do women wait more than men, she asks, and then inventories all those things we wait for: money, weather, love, the plumber, the lover, the estranged friend to forgive us, our hair to grow, letters to arrive, toast to brown, medical tests, the pain in the shoulder to cease, and how we may wait differently indoors than we do outdoors. And it is all true: The things we wait for and the kinds of waiting they invite are all infinitely varied. Having said that, I also think how strange it is that the same quality can be in such demand for two such different enterprises: finding the patience to live with what you do have and learning the patience to wait for what you don't.

Which brings me to realize that it is impossible to consider patience and not write about people and the people for whom you wait—sometimes willingly, sometimes because it is the only thing we can do; sometimes with faith, sometimes without any sort of faith at all; sometimes only for a short time, but often for a very long time. Most of what you wait for is elusive, indeterminate, fugitive, operating with a schedule of its own. But waiting for people—whether you are waiting for someone to sign a contract, a friend to come for dinner, a child to grow older, your husband to come to his senses—is always waiting for something unknown, unpredictable. It is different from waiting for anything else, because you are waiting not for a train to roll in, a season to turn, an orchid to bloom, water to boil, soup to cool—all of which occur at predictable intervals. Instead, you are waiting for something with a will of its own. You are waiting for some puzzle of human behavior to reveal itself, waiting to comprehend how the metal rings can be fastened together or the silk scarves unknotted, and even if you are not familiar with that particular puzzle, you are forced to admit that the collection of puzzles at large is known to you because you have your own.

And I think, too, that when we wait for other people—to do something, to say something, to come into the room and sit at the table or to leave the table—we have some intuitive knowledge that we may find ourselves waiting forever. When my sister and I were children, my father often traveled to Japan. The postcards we received from him frequently were of Mount Fuji. I saved them and, over the years, acquired stacks and stacks of these postcards of the sacred mountain, seemingly from every angle, in full sunlight and shrouded in mist, when the sky was blue or gray or peach colored, at dawn and dusk, in every season, from afar and up close, behind the Shinto shrine at Hakone, across a blue lake from the village of Nihondaira, through a grove of pines and across Lake Kawaguchi.

I think of all of these now as images that decorate some giant avenue of waiting, the way the portraits of generations of ancestors hang in the hallways that lead from one great room to another in English manors. Though nothing more than small pictures printed on glossy paper, they offered landscapes of patience, and I know that if I were to visit Japan now and see the snow-capped mountain for myself, it would never be as immense as it appeared on those little three-by-five postcards. The way these small mountains arrived week after week clarified how absence often registers as a matter of repetition, a loss that is reiterated one day after the next.

But then there are times when you find yourself waiting only for you. Maybe you have sent some little part of yourself out into the world on an expedition. You have written an article, an essay, a book. You have written a letter, or met with someone, or had lunch, or a drink. You have done something or said something to someone, or you have given something to someone. And now you are waiting to see what comes of it—what that part of yourself that has ventured out comes back with, whether it has been changed or even transformed. And it almost always comes back with some new color or shape or texture, some souvenir from the outing. Maybe it is some bit of ephemera, the equivalent of a book of matches or a cocktail napkin. Or maybe it is something more substantial: a table made from exotic wood and carved with ornate motifs, or a coat with some new pattern of threads, and beads, and buttons, and bits of fur and ribbon. But, at times, there will be nothing at all. That bit of yourself will come back empty handed from an excursion that has proven pointless. Sometimes, I think that waiting for yourself is the most difficult because it is by your own arrangement.

What remains a puzzle to me is why, when waiting for any thing or person, we tend to underestimate inaction. Surely inaction is one of patience's most intimate yet unrecognized consorts, shifting unexpectedly between expectation, anticipation, and contemplation. Expectancy, Kierkegaard tells us, "is like a good word in the right place. Like a golden apple in a silver bowl," a statement that also suggests there is nothing economical about patience; like the alabaster clock on my mantle, it is strictly a luxury good.

Jason Barger, a business consultant and frequent flyer, came to much the same conclusion recently. Barger took it upon himself to spend an entire week in that vast museum of impatience— the American airport—keeping a diary of the experience. Barger's diary, which he published as *Step Back from the Baggage Claim: Change the World, Start at the Airport*, documents the race to get off the plane, then sprint through the terminal, then rush to baggage claim, only to stand there *waiting*. He writes convincingly of embracing "the quiet moments an airplane seat offers us. When the ding sends most of us into a frenzy, I am going to sit still."

Kids have some implicit knowledge about the value of this unclaimed time. I remember the significance riding the school bus took on when my sons were in first grade. What happened in the classroom when they got to school mattered—they learned to fasten letters to words and words to meaning, to add and to subtract, to work at a table with another small child, to cut the shape of countries out of colored paper and fit them together on a map with other countries made of colored paper. Still, what happened on the school bus was more important. "Mom, the bus was where all the action was," one of the boys told me later when he was a teenager. Those thirty minutes on the bus allowed for unregimented time and unregulated behavior. How you chose your seat, whom you sat with and spoke to, whether you traded lunch, did homework, or just gazed out the window were all momentous decisions to my six-year-old boys. I think the kids were on to something: Getting from here to there, whether it is on a yellow school bus or 747 jet, offers open, unclaimed time with a range of choices that have a value of their own.

Inaction has its own rhythm, its silence, stillness, all those varied pauses in which it is possible to find there are differences between idleness and inertia. Rarely do we decide to wait. Almost always it seems to be something enforced upon us by circumstances, by people, by weather—a lengthy download, a friend who is late for lunch, a snowstorm that keeps us housebound. Yet, in an age when we never seem to have enough time, you would think we would put these snags in the daily schedule to use.

My friend Michael does just this. "I am extraordinarily impatient," he told me, "and so I simply make sure I am never kept waiting." By which he means he always has something to do, whether it is reading a book, doing a crossword puzzle, or drafting a legal argument. He has found a way of ordering thought, or perhaps of simply giving precedence to one thought over another. Such a strategy can transform the experience of waiting from a passive exercise to an active one, involving *choice*. In the introduction to *Rapt*, Gallagher remarks on the power of turning something that is demanded or extracted from us into something that is chosen: "That your experience largely depends on the material objects and mental subjects that you choose to pay attention to or ignore is not an imaginative notion but a physiological fact."

Which brings me to Robert Ryman, whose paintings are always solid white, whether on canvas, linen, fiberglass, steel, copper, aluminum composites, or paper that is ripped or intact. Composed in a variety of strokes and gestures and textures in gradations of ivory, marble, or chalk, these little blank patches are fastened to the wall with brackets, screws, nails, and tape, in a full catalog of the tenacity with which even the most imperceptible thoughts, impressions, and desires manage to attach themselves to our subconscious. At times sensuous and at times austere, the white surface recedes or advances. Sometimes, it just lies flat. At other times, it resonates with depth and light.

Like the time between anticipated events, the space between things is never static. I look now at the snow between the trees. Like some improvisational archive of Ryman paintings, the white surfaces are under constant revision. A single warm day and a freeze at night are all it takes for the dry powder of the new snow to become a brittle, glittering crust. The patterns of tracks in the snow—the texture of my boots, the hoofprints left by the deer, the calligraphy left by the hawk that seems to have found its prey here as well—all of these have lost their imprint of immediacy and become expanded, indelible. The cycles of thawing, melting, and refreezing have magnified and deepened their incisions in the snow into a steadfast hieroglyph that will remain until some shift in weather—be it more snow, sun, or rain—occurs, and all of it will simply vanish again.

And even if it seems certain the color has fled, you are likely to find it again in increments. In the early morning, the inky blue of the night sky that seemed to seep into the snow continues to linger there, while in late afternoon, for a few moments, the snow takes on the pink glaze of the sky. Its radiance is not so vivid as the maple leaves in October, but there is a glow nonetheless. And from time to time, too, the blank slate of snow becomes animate with drifting shadows, and I am reminded of how the space between things has a color, texture, and quiet momentum of its own.

As the air warms, the snow recedes in quiet increments, ceding only a few inches each day to the grass and leaves beneath. The outline of the remaining snow changes each morning as it seeps into the ground, evaporating—sublimating—slowly and in unpredictable patterns. On some mornings I find that it has melted, pooled, and then turned to ice. At such times, it seems as though there isn't much of a difference between waiting for something to come and waiting for something to go; both often happen in bits and pieces.

Time seems to accelerate as we get older, James Gleick notes in *Faster*. "Perhaps that is partly because the end is near," he writes. "Psychologists have isolated a 'gradient of tension' to measure the shift in our sense of time as we approach a critical point—the end of a basketball game, a journey, a book, a millennium, a lifetime." It seems hardwired in us to experience the rush of time as we age, to recognize childhood as a vast temporal territory while our adult years slip by instantaneously. This kind of acceleration is different from speed-dating and fifteen-minute mortgage approvals; it is rather a hastening, a kind of dire quickening of that interior calendar we all have, when that space between things seems diminished and when the rhythm of expectation and experience is necessarily recalibrated. And when the compression of time that comes with the information age is brought into the mix, that acceleration can visit us as some impossible infringement. Small wonder that Gleick, one of the country's foremost science writers, was drawn to the subject of speed and its effects on the human psyche.

I wonder if patience eventually offers us a kind of reset button—one equipped with active and passive options, settings capable of recognizing both that rush of time and all its pauses. I wonder if this button is equipped with some inclusive measuring system that accommodates both an appreciation for time and an indifference toward it, a system that does the work of the digital readout in the corner of my computer monitor while acknowledging that imperceptible interior leaning that stills the alabaster clock on my mantel. Maybe this reset button allows us to recognize weight, tone value, and texture where they are not apparent—and, most of all, helps us to perceive what is distant and what is close.

Afterword

"Oh, patience," says my friend Sally, laughing. "I always get it mixed up with forgiveness." She told me this when we were in our friend Polly's pottery studio. I was holding a large green celadon bowl, and she was looking at a shelf lined with blue and white bowls of varying sizes. On the table in front of us were an immense cobalt platter the size of a shield; flowerpots decorated with purple irises; salad bowls decorated with fuchsias; cake plates imprinted with leaves, pine needles, and garlands of lace; and mugs and cups of varying shapes and sizes.

Throughout the conversation, we were picking up these bowls and vases and pots and plates, all of them artifacts of graciousness. Some of them seemed almost to illustrate what she was saying, which is that patience and forgiveness are both acts of generosity.

Both also require some degree of trust and graceful acceptance, and both may also be contingent upon the passage of time. Both, Sally added, "demand a letting go, or more accurately 'not biting the hook,' what the Tibetan Buddhists call *shenpa*, or attachment, the root cause of aggression and craving."

This conversation in the studio comes back to me often. It comes back to me early in the morning when I am waiting for the coffee to brew, when I am waiting in line at the grocery store, when I am on the platform waiting for the commuter train, or when I am sitting in traffic. It comes back to me at night when I am waiting for sleep to come, and during the wet, muddy month of March, when I am eager for the first crocuses, snowdrops, and daffodils to emerge from last year's leaves. And when I am waiting for all those things for which I don't even really know I am waiting. In other words, the conversation comes back to me at all those times when I, too, would like to confuse patience with forgiveness.

But patience *is* a way of forgiving—time, circumstance, what has happened, what hasn't happened, what may or may not come to you. And Buddhist scholar Robert A. F. Thurman would see Sally's confusion as a moment of bright clarity. In his meditation on transcendent patience, he speaks of irritation, injury, and harm as being occasions to practice endurance, forbearance, and forgiveness. He writes of entering "the land of patience as active forgiveness. Joyfully, ecstatically, we celebrate our initial freedom from fear of suffering by going beyond patience as endurance and as forbearance and enter patience as nonretaliation and forgiveness. This is the antechamber of the temple of compassion."

That antechamber seems distant. The closest I've come to it was that November morning in Polly's pottery studio, the shelves piled high with all their different bowls, platters, pots, plates, and cups. I know now that each has its own measure of sufficiency, and that what is enough can be measured by so many different shapes and sizes.

Acknowledgments

I am deeply grateful to all those who had a hand in this, with thanks especially to Albert LaFarge, Carl Lehmann-Haupt, Steven Magnuson, Allan Fallow, Jennifer Williams, Melanie Madden, and Meredith Hale.

Index

INDEX